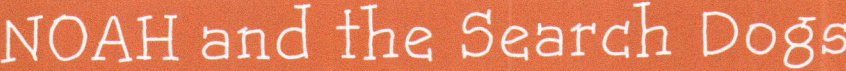

NOAH and the Search Dogs

The Story of BOO

Patricia Abrams

the Peppertree Press
Sarasota, Florida

In Memory of Boo

It came to me that every time I lose a dog, they take a piece of my heart with them, and every new dog who comes into my life gifts me with a piece of their heart. If I live long enough, all the components of my heart will be dog and I will become as generous and loving as they are.

Copyright © Patricia Abrams, 2012

All rights reserved. Published by the Peppertree Press, LLC. the Peppertree Press and associated logos are trademarks of the Peppertree Press, LLC.
No part of this publication may be reproduced, stored in a retrieval system, transmitted in any form or by any means, electronic, mechanical, photocopying, recording, or otherwise, without prior written permission of the publisher and author/illustrator. Graphic design by Rebecca Barbier.

Photography by the following contributors: Flash and Company, Alan Veres, Linc and Jon Hay, Joseph Abrams, Tami Treadway, and Sharpe - Taborsky

For information regarding permission, call 941-922-2662 or contact us at our website: www.peppertreepublishing.com or write to: the Peppertree Press, LLC.
Attention: Publisher
1269 First Street, Suite 7
Sarasota, Florida 34236

ISBN: 978-1-61493-104-1
Library of Congress Number: 2012915901
Printed in the U.S.A.
Printed September 2012

Tami Treadway and K-9 Boo

This book is dedicated to the Community Foundation and the Wilson-Wood Foundation for their belief in making dreams come true by offering charitable support and recognizing the importance of building a strong and safe community.

This book is dedicated to our community's children so they can learn to be safe and appreciate the great services that search and rescue dogs provide.

This book is dedicated to Sarasota K-9 Search and Rescue handlers and their canines for providing their communities the service to educate children and finding the lost and bringing them home.

Adopt A Pet, Save A Life

boo

I was treated cruelly by my old owner and now I'm looking for a real friend. I'm a two year old black lab beagle mix with a lot of spunk and love to give. I'd love to play ball and swim with you. I'm also the perfect size for any home, especially yours.

It was a warm day in Florida where families enjoyed their day at the beach soaking up the warm sun and finding seashells along the shore. It was great to build sandcastles and the surf filled the castle moats with water. Children were laughing and running, flying kites high in the sky. When it was time to leave, the families would venture into town, go get an ice cream and window shop.

But on this same beautiful day, a mean man was also in town with his small black dog. All the townspeople heard a terrible screaming and watched in horror at how this man mistreated his dog. This man was so mean that he kicked the dog and threw him against a dumpster so hard that he just lay on the ground lifeless. The townspeople were so upset for the dog, but thankfully Deputy Kost saw this act of cruelty and took the dog away from the man.

He arrested him for not making good choices. It is against the law to hurt people and animals. The policeman did not know the dog's name and said, "You are going to be okay, boy." He picked him up and wrapped him in a blanket and took him to the doctor so he could be treated. The dog's body was badly bruised and his feelings were hurt that someone he loved could ever treat him like that. He kept thinking, "Where will I live now? Who will be my mommy and daddy? I am scared and all alone."

The veterinarian checked the dog all over and gave him some medicine to help him feel better. Then a white van came to the doctor's office and picked up this black dog and took him to the Sarasota Animal Services shelter where he met a lady named Tami. She was going to take care of him. She named him Boo because his coat was jet black and so shiny. His coat reminded her of Halloween. She took Boo into her office and talked to him for quite a long time and told him about the shelter and where he was going to stay. Tami said all the dogs that live here are looking for their forever homes with a family where they can be loved and cared for. She told Boo that he had to rest and get well and she would make sure that he was taken care of.

Boo was assigned his own kennel. He had a blanket for his bed and bowl of clean water. He could go inside or outside of his kennel. There was a tall oak tree that gave him a cool breeze on his face. Sitting on the tree's branches were two squirrels that looked at him all concerned and chattered a song. Boo loved to go outside of his kennel because the warm sun shone on his fur. It made his bruises feel better.

Boo talked with the other shelter dogs and listened to their stories. All the stories he heard were so sad. The shelter dogs wanted a home and a family. Every time people came to look at the dogs, they would get all excited and say, "Look at me, look at me! I'm a great dog to take home." But Boo stayed quiet because he secretly fell in love with Tami. When she came to visit him, his stubby tail would wag so fast and he would jump the kennel door so high to get her attention. Tami and him would take walks and play ball together. She would talk with him and build up his confidence. Tami would tell him he was a great dog many times of the day. This made Boo feel special.

One day Tami brought Boo inside her office to have some quality time. She had to tell Boo that he would have to be at the shelter for a long time until the man that hurt him was convicted of the crime that he did. Tami made sure that Boo understood that he did nothing wrong. This was not his fault. She made sure he understood that she would be with him every day and they would wait together until he would find his forever home.

The days, weeks, and months went by and Boo and Tami passed the time by playing ball in the green cool grass, going for long walks and having the best talks in her office. The nights were very lonely and Boo just curled up in his bed dreaming of the day he would have a family. Now Tami had heard about a new Search and Rescue team in Sarasota looking for volunteers and dogs to search for missing people. She was very interested in joining the group but she did not have a dog yet.

So one day she was playing with Boo and she asked him, "Boo would you like to be a search and rescue dog"? And Boo answered, "What is a search and rescue dog?" So Tami said, "You have to use your nose and smell for the lost people and work very hard to find them." Boo thought about this and turned around and said to Tami, "Well, you rescued me when I was lost so I think I can pay it forward and rescue people that are lost and bring them home". Boo jumped up high into Tami's arms and she said," Boo would you like to be my dog? Would you like to live with me and have this be your forever home?" Boo barked and barked and ran in the green grass and said, "Yes! Yes, I want to be your dog forever!" So Tami adopted Boo and they joined Sarasota K-9 Search and Rescue Team.

Boo was introduced to Tami's house where he had his own comfortable bed, clean water and good food to eat. She bought him lots of new toys and his own special name tag for his collar. Boo felt so special because he never had a home like this one. When Boo discovered Tami's bedroom, he found his own bed. It had his name on it. It was so fluffy and comfortable. He tried it out and it smelled of his new home. Boo was so excited that he did not have to sleep on the hard kennel concrete floor anymore. Boo was feeling better about life and he was ready to start his new journey.

Tami took Boo to the veterinarian and Dr. Laurie checked him out from head to paws. Dr. Laurie said, "Boo, your body is healed and you are healthy." So Dr. Laurie signed the important papers that Boo could begin his search and rescue training. Boo jumped and spun circles because he was so happy.

So Tami drove Boo to training. Boo met Noah for the first time. They both smelled each other and Noah said, "Hi, Boo, welcome to the team." Boo sat and offered Noah his paw and said, "Nice to meet you, Noah. I am so excited to be here. I promise I will do an excellent job."

Noah and Boo became best friends instantly. They were partners in the field. Wherever you saw Noah, there was Boo carrying a special stick and the both of them were playing tug of war. Noah always watched out for Boo because he knew that Boo was a little nervous around strange men. He always wanted to stay as close to Tami as he could. Noah understood what Boo was going through, but he did not want Boo to be worried about this. He wanted Boo to be totally free and become a leader in his life.

Noah and Boo took a long walk together and Noah said, "Boo, you need to forgive the bad man that hurt you. You need to just let it go. He cannot hurt you anymore. "Boo just looked at him and said, "How can I forgive someone that didn't love me when I loved him so much?" Noah said, "You are safe and loved now, Boo. Your job is to be courageous and be a leader. You need to keep training so you can find the lost children and people that need to come home. If you keep thinking about the bad thoughts, the good that you do will never shine on your face."

So Boo thought about those words and he looked up at Tami and said to himself, I am going to forgive that bad man because I am saved and I can make a difference in so many lives. With that all said and done, Boo and Noah did their very best favorite thing in the world—they went swimming.

In order for Boo to learn how to search, Tami had to find a great reward toy for Boo. All the search dogs had them and it made them very happy to get their favorite toy when they did something great. Tami saw Boo always looking up at the trees when the squirrels were chattering. She asked Boo, "Do you like the squirrels? He said, "I do like them. They talked to me when I was sick in the kennel, but I couldn't understand what they were saying. I am very interested in knowing them."

So Tami went to the store and bought Boo his own toy squirrel. He was so excited that he gently put that toy squirrel in his mouth and bragged that he had his own reward. So every time Boo found a lost person, Tami gave him his squirrel and he raised his head and showed everyone on the team that he did an excellent job!

Boo trained very hard and became an excellent search and rescue dog. He was very fast when he searched for people. The team members called him Pocket Rocket and the Black Tornado. Boo said to Noah, "Why do I have so many names? My name is Boo."

Noah wagged his tail and said, "Nicknames are good, Boo. My nickname is Palmetto Buster." Boo sat with his ears up and said, "What kind of name is that?" Noah barked and ran to the edge of the woods and showed Boo how his strength helped him run right through these big plants. Noah came back panting and said, "Boo, your nickname means that you are fast. You can find the lost and come back and show Tami where they are in minutes."

So Boo put his ears down and tucked his back legs in and said to Noah, "Watch this!" He ran as fast as he could into the woods and came back to Noah with his tongue hanging on the side and said, "I love my nickname. I am fast. I am the Black Tornado!"

Tami and Boo became inseparable. They were a dedicated team. Boo became a strong leader and he helped Tami train other search and rescue dogs. He was obedient and trustworthy. Boo always focused on his teammates and did what was best for the mission. He was committed in the duty to serve others, while caring for all life.

Boo had made a promise that he would never forget the shelter dogs that became his friends. Tami and Boo gave a lot of talks to children and adults on how to care for dogs and the importance of adopting a pet from a shelter. Boo felt his journey in life was to give back for his own life. So he continued to save the lost and find homes for the lonely animals in the shelter.

Boo's character word is loyalty. He was so proud of his search and rescue vest that when he put it on, there was nothing that he would not do for Tami and the team. He would work all day and night and he would not whimper or whine. He was so proud he could honor his life with saving another life. He became the poster child for many organizations and served his community for twelve years.

Noah always reminded him that if you don't know, don't go and for this he never left his mother's side and he did not have butterflies in his tummy again. When he went and did talks with the children, he made Tami tell them this important safety

rule so they would always feel safe too. Boo loved hearing his story told and he wanted all the children to know that if they were hurt by anyone, they needed to tell someone right away. No person or animal deserves to be hurt. Everyone deserves to be loved and cared for.

When you are loved by a family and taken care of, you have the opportunity to do great things in your life, because you have trust and belief that you can be anything you want to be.

Tami had received an invitation in the mail to bring Boo to a party. This special night was to honor Boo in the first annual Florida Veterinary Medical Association Pet Hall of Fame. Boo was going to get an award for being brave and courageous in his fight to stop animals from being abused and to also overcome his own abuse in becoming a search and rescue dog.

This was a huge event. Tami told Boo all about the award and Boo was thrilled. He had a bath, had his toenails done, brushed his teeth and wore his brand new collar that matched his leash. He then put on his search and rescue vest and he was all dressed to go to his party. Boo walked with his head held up high and jumped up on his chair. The program began and the people said so many nice things about him. So many photographers were taking his picture and the lights were stinging his eyes.

But when Boo looked up at Tami and saw her tears of joy, he called her Mom for the first time. Boo raised his paw to Tami's chest and said, "Mom, why are you crying? Are you okay?" Tami reached down and picked up Boo and hugged him and said, "I love you so much, Boo. I am very proud of you." Boo knew that he really belonged to a family now and he had the confidence to continue his important work.

Tami wanted to expand Boo's search training and teach him more information on how to be a better search and rescue dog. So she applied to a summer camp for Boo. Tami asked Boo, "Do you want to go with me to West Virginia?" Boo sat and looked directly into her eyes and said, "What is West Virginia?" Tami's voice got very excited and said, "We would go on a plane and travel to a state that has mountains, streams, and a big forest. It will be so fun, Boo."

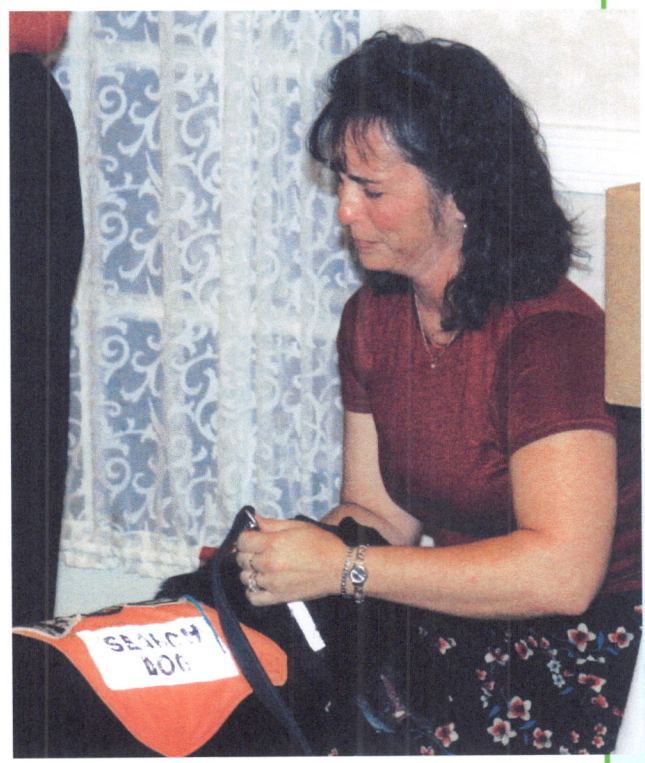

So Boo jumped up high and ran in circles and said, "Of course, I want to go. I have never been on a plane or seen a mountain. This summer camp is a great idea. When are we going?" Tami petted Boo and said, "We will go next week. We have a lot to do to get ready."

Boo was so excited to think about his travels to a faraway place. He would meet new friends and learn so much about search work. Boo watched Tami pack his and her bags. She was bringing all the good toys and food. This is so exciting. It was the day to go to summer camp and Tami loaded the car and put Boo's search and rescue vest on. They drove to the airport and Tami seemed a little nervous about the trip. Boo was walking through the airport with his head held high and did his dog strut as they were getting to where their plane would take off.

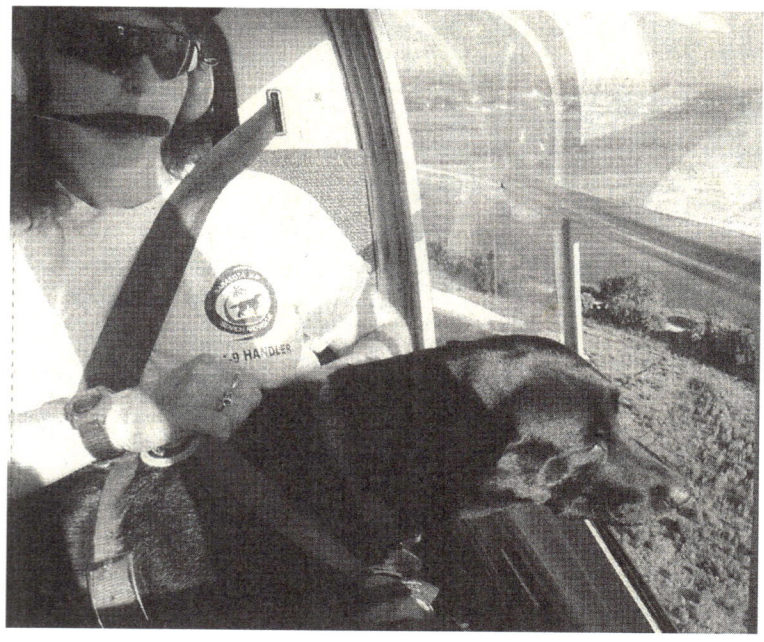

Boo felt a strange feeling coming from his leash. He never felt this feeling before. He looked up at his mom and she was holding him tight. Boo put his paw on her chest and said, "Everything okay, Mom?" Tami answered, "Boo, I am a little nervous about flying in a plane. I do not like heights." Boo thought about this for a while and said, "Mom, we will be okay. Just follow me."

With that, Boo stood up and took over and walked in front of Tami all the way into the plane and they sat down looking out the window. The airplane started down the runway and Boo felt that tight feeling on his leash again. Boo said, "Mom, look at the beautiful clouds. We can almost touch them. Let's play a game of picture clouds." "What game is that, Boo?" Boo looked at her with his ear tilted and said, "The game where we find faces in the clouds and we say what they are."

So that's what Tami and Boo did the whole way to West Virginia. They played the cloud game. Boo was very happy that his leash was not tight anymore. When the plane landed, he went outside and saw the big mountains and felt the coolness on his face. He looked at his mom and said, "This is going to be the best summer camp in the world."

Boo worked hard for the whole week. He learned about the different forests to run in to find people and to jump rocks across the babbling brook. Boo met so many friends, even two eagles that flew over him while he was searching. He spent the entire week watching his mom learn how to teach the other search dogs lessons when they got back to Florida. It was great! Boo couldn't wait to get back home and tell Noah all of his adventures.

When summer camp was over, it was back to work as usual. But this time, Boo had so many stories to share with everyone. Boo showed all the search dogs the new way of training, so they could locate the missing person faster. Everyone was busy practicing and talking about it. All his hard work paid off, because it made everyone stronger on the team.

Since Boo had been away, he asked his mom if he could go to visit the shelter dogs and give them a cookie. Tami said, "Okay, Boo, you can go to work with me today." So Boo picked out the cookies and gave all the shelter dogs one and had a great visit with each of them. He gave them a smile, a paw, and promise that they would all get their forever homes. They just needed to be patient. He played with them in the green grass and they chased each other around until they were tired. Before you knew it, he had to leave to go home. Boo said goodbye to everyone and he jumped in his mom's car to go home and have dinner.

As Tami and Boo were driving home, Boo looked at his mom and said, "Do you know we have been together for twelve years?" Tami took one hand off the steering wheel and said to Boo, "We will be together forever!" Boo was so happy and content that he put his head on his mom's shoulder.

When Boo got home, he had a great meal and watched some TV with his mom and decided it was time for bed. Boo went into the bedroom and settled in his bed. He made about three turns before the bed was just right and he closed his eyes and began to dream.

Boo's dream took him to search the clouds and he jumped each and every one of them as he had jumped the rocks on the streams. He wanted to get to the tops of the clouds and when he did he found this beautiful bridge. Boo landed on it and looked around and he saw the most beautiful colors that reminded him of his life. He saw the green and it was the green grass he was used to running in playing ball with Tami. He saw the yellow that reminded him of the sun that warmed his black fur when he was hurt. He gazed into the blue color that reminded him of the sky when he watched the eagles fly over him. Boo looked at the purple color, which reminded him of the wildflowers in Deer Prairie Creek where he loved to train and search. He also found the orange, which reminded him of Halloween and all the kids would knock on the door and say, "Trick or treat!" Boo would come out and say, "BOO!" The gold color reminded Boo of the Spirit Award medal he received from his K-9 partners for his determination to leave his paw prints in the sand so others could follow and finish his dream.

He stared at the colors for a long time and turned his head only to see that the clouds had blown away. Then a teardrop left his eye and landed on Tami's cheek. When Tami awoke in the morning, it was raining, and the most beautiful rainbow was outside. That was her gift from Boo.

Boo wants all of you to know that serving mankind is the best service you can do for your community. His wish is to continue the training of future search and rescue dogs so the team will keep on forever doing their great work in finding the lost and for everyone to find it in their hearts to adopt a shelter animal and give them a forever home because everyone needs a best friend and a family.

Giving a rescue dog a home will not change the world,
But for that one dog their world will change forever.

Picture drawn by Eriq Masters, age 7,
2nd grade, Imagine School. North Port, FL — Tami Treadway's grandson

Boo's Glossary of Words

Animal Shelter: Safe place where trained people care for stray and homeless pets to find homes for them.

Adoption: To be accepted into a family and loved as their own child or animal.

Convicted: Judge has sentenced one to be guilty.

Veterinarian: Animal doctor.

Palmetto: Tropical plant having fan-shaped leaves.

Search Mission: When the search team comes together to find the lost person.

West Virginia: The 35th state of the United States.

Babbling Brook: Little stream with pebbles in it and makes a bubbly, gurgling sound that is very relaxing.

Deer Prairie Creek: Special place in Sarasota, Florida, where the search dogs learn to search. In the springtime, it has the most beautiful wildflowers that grow there.

www.ingramcontent.com/pod-product-compliance
Ingram Content Group UK Ltd.
Pitfield, Milton Keynes, MK11 3LW, UK
UKHW060132240426
12048UKWH00002B/4